JIM CROCE
FOR UKULELE

Cover photo courtesy Ingrid Croce

ISBN 978-1-4950-2834-2

HAL•LEONARD®
CORPORATION

7777 W. BLUEMOUND RD. P.O. BOX 13819 MILWAUKEE, WI 53213

In Australia Contact:
Hal Leonard Australia Pty. Ltd.
4 Lentara Court
Cheltenham, Victoria, 3192 Australia
Email: ausadmin@halleonard.com.au

Visit Hal Leonard Online at
www.halleonard.com

Age

Words and Music by Jim Croce and Ingrid Croce

Additional Lyrics

2. Once I had myself a million, now I've only got a dime.
   The difference don't seem quite so bad today.
   With a nickel or a million, I was searching all the time
   For something that I never lost or left behind.

3. Now I'm in my second circle and I'm headin' for the top.
   I've learned a lot of things along the way.
   I'll be careful while I'm climbin' 'cause it hurts a lot to drop,
   And when you're down nobody gives a damn anyway.

Alabama Rain

Words and Music by Jim Croce

1. La - zy days in mid - Ju - ly, ___ coun - try Sun - day
2., 3. *See additional lyrics*

morn - in's. ___ Dust - y haze on sum - mer high - ways,

sweet mag - no - lia call - in'. ___ But now and then, I

find my - self ___ think - in' of the days that we were

walk - in' in the Al - a - bam - a rain. ___

4

Additional Lyrics

2. Drive-in movies Friday nights, drinkin' beer and laughin'.
   Somehow things were always right; I just don't know what happened.

3. On a dusty mid-July, country summer's evenin',
   A weepin' willow sang its lullaby and shared our secret.

Dreamin' Again

Words and Music by Jim Croce

1. Don't you know I _____ had a dream _____ last night _____

(2., 3.) *See additional lyrics*

that you were here with me, _____ ly - in' by my side _

_____ so _____ soft and warm. _____ And we

talked a while _ and shared a smile, _____ and then we shared the dawn. _

_____ But when I woke up, oh, my dream, _____ it was gone. _

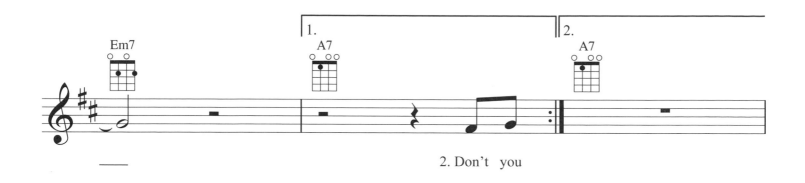

2. Don't you

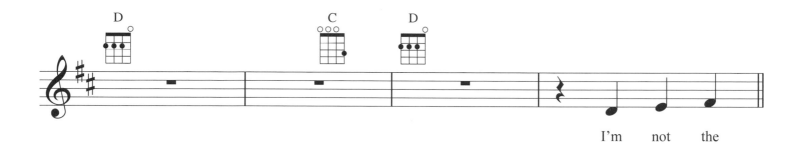

I'm not the

Bridge

same; can you blame ___ me? Is it hard to un - der - stand? _

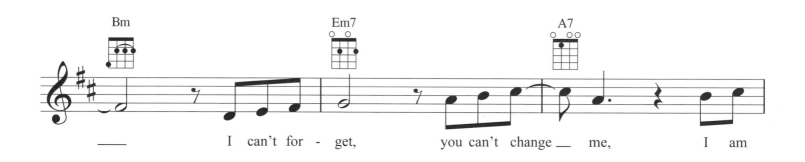

___ I can't for - get, you can't change ___ me, I am

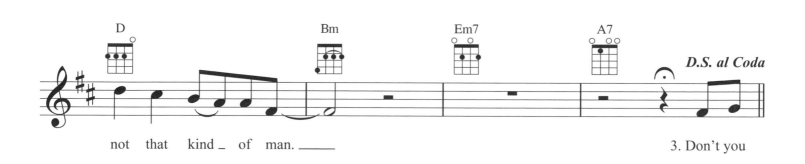

D.S. al Coda

not that kind _ of man. ___ 3. Don't you

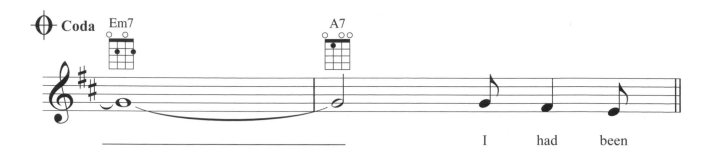

Coda Em7   A7

I   had   been

Outro

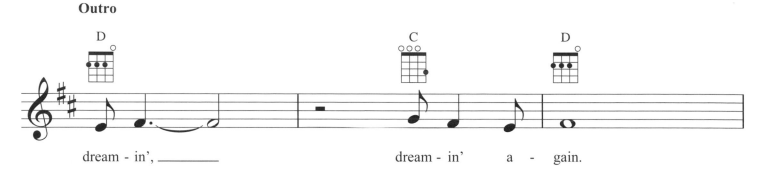

D   C   D

dream - in', _____   dream - in'   a - gain.

C   D   C

I   had   been dream - in', _____   dream - in'   a -

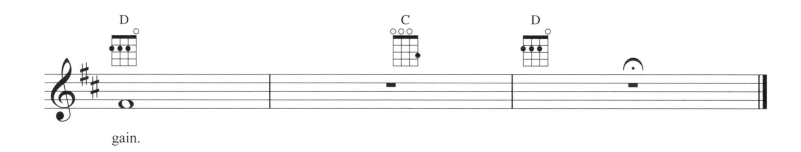

D   C   D

gain.

Additional Lyrics

2. Don't you know I had a dream last night and you were here with me,
Lyin' by my side so soft and warm.
And you said you'd thought it over, you said that you were comin' home.
But when I woke up, oh, my dream, it was gone.

3. Don't you know I had a dream last night and everything was still.
You were by my side so soft and warm.
And I dreamed that we were lovers in the lemon-scented rain,
But when I woke up, oh, I found that again... *(To Coda)*

Bad, Bad Leroy Brown

Words and Music by Jim Croce

-town la - dies call him "tree-top lov - er," all the

men just call him "Sir." ___ And he's bad, ___ bad

Le - roy Brown, ___ the bad-dest man ___ in the whole damned town; ___

bad-der than old King Kong ___ and mean-er than a junk-yard dog. ___

1., 2.
___ 2. Now, Le -
3. Well, Fri -

3.
___ 4. Well, the two ___ men took to fight-

- in', and when they pulled them from the floor, ___

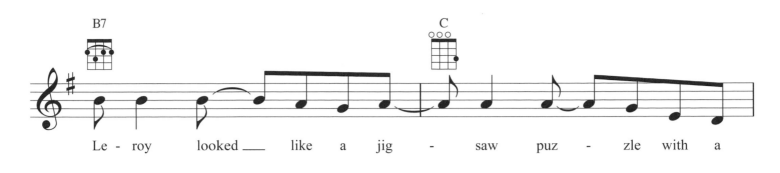

Le - roy looked ___ like a jig - saw puz - zle with a

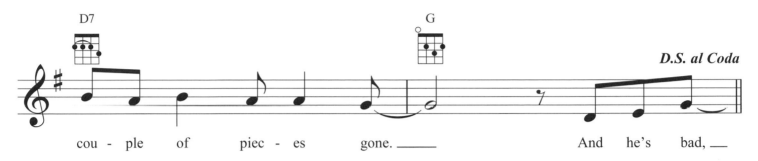

D.S. al Coda

cou - ple of piec - es gone. ___ And he's bad, ___

Coda

Outro

___ Yes, you were bad - der than old King Kong, ___

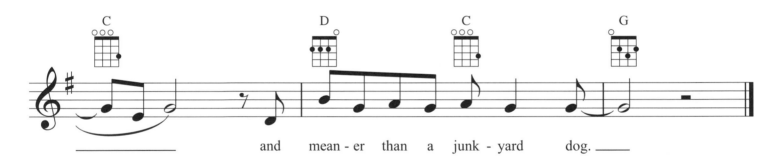

___ and mean - er than a junk - yard dog. ___

Additional Lyrics

2. Now, Leroy, he a gambler and he like his fancy clothes,
   And he like to wave his diamond rings
   In front of everybody's nose.
   He got a custom Continental, he got a Eldorado, too.
   He got a thirty-two gun in his pocket for fun,
   He got a razor in his shoe.

3. Well, Friday 'bout a week ago, Leroy shootin' dice.
   And at the edge of the bar sat a girl name of Doris
   And, oh, that girl looked nice.
   Well, he cast his eyes upon her and the trouble soon began,
   And Leroy Brown, he learned a lesson
   'Bout messin' with the wife of a jealous man.

I Got a Name

Words by Norman Gimbel
Music by Charles Fox

Verse
Moderately, in 2

1. Like the pine trees lin - ing the wind - ing road, ___
2., 4. *See additional lyrics*
3. *Instrumental*

I've got a name, ___ I've got a name. _

Like the sing - ing bird _

___ and the croak - ing toad, I've got a name, _

To Coda 1

___ I've got a name. _

Instrumental ends

Additional Lyrics

2. Like the north wind whistlin' down the sky, I've got a song, I've got a song.
    Like the whippoorwill and the baby's cry, I've got a song, I've got a song,

Pre-Chorus: And I carry it with me and I sing it loud;
    If it gets me nowhere, I'll go there proud.

4. Like the fool I am and I'll always be, I've got a dream, I've got a dream.
    They can change their minds but they can't change me. I've got a dream, I've got a dream.

Pre-Chorus: Oh, I know I could share it if you'd want me to.
    If you're goin' my way, I'll go with you.

14

A Long Time Ago

Words and Music by Jim Croce

I'll Have to Say
I Love You in a Song

Words and Music by Jim Croce

First note

Verse
Moderately fast

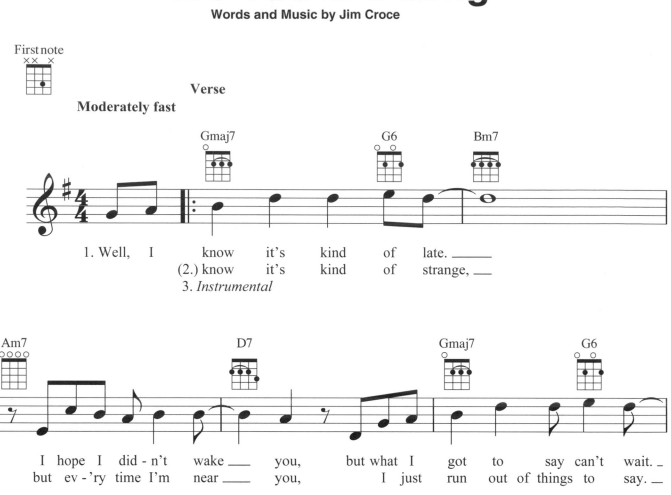

1. Well, I know it's kind of late. _____
(2.) know it's kind of strange, _____
3. *Instrumental*

I hope I did - n't wake _____ you, but what I got to say can't wait. _
but ev - 'ry time I'm near _____ you, I just run out of things to say. _

_____ I know you'd un - der - stand. _____
_____ I know you'd un - der - stand. _____
Instrumental ends

𝄋 Chorus

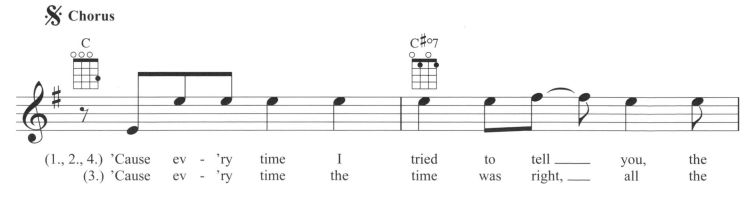

(1., 2., 4.) 'Cause ev - 'ry time I tried to tell _____ you, the
(3.) 'Cause ev - 'ry time the time was right, _____ all the

It Doesn't Have to Be That Way

Words and Music by Jim Croce

Lover's Cross

Words and Music by Jim Croce

Additional Lyrics

2. Yes, I really got to hand it to you; 'cause, girl you really tried.
But for every time that we spent laughin', there were two times that I cried.

Chorus: And you were tryin' to make me your martyr, and that's the one thing I just couldn't do.
'Cause, baby, I can't hang upon no lover's cross for you.

3. So, I'll hope that you can find another who can take what I could not.
He'll have to be a super guy or maybe a super god.

Chorus: 'Cause I never was much of a martyr before and I ain't 'bout to start nothin' new.
And, baby, I can't hang upon no lover's cross for you.

New York's Not My Home

Words and Music by Jim Croce

1. Well, things were spin-nin' 'round me and all my
2. *See additional lyrics*

thoughts were cloud - y, and I had be - gun to doubt all the things

that were me. *(Instrumental)* Been in so

man - y plac - es, you know I've run so man - y rac - es,

and looked in - to the emp - ty fac - es of the peo - ple of the night, and

Chorus

some-thing is just ___ not right.

{ 'Cause I know that I got-ta get out ___ of here; }
{ That's the rea-son that I got-ta get out ___ of here; }

I'm so a - lone. ___ Don't you know that I

got - ta get out ___ of here, 'cause New York's not ___ my home. ___

Outro

(Instrumental)

Additional Lyrics

2. Though all the streets are crowded, there's something strange about it.
   I lived there 'bout a year and I never once felt at home.
   I thought I'd make the big time, I learned a lot of lessons awful quick, and now I'm
   Tellin' you that they were not the nice kind, and it's been so long since I have felt fine.

One Less Set of Footsteps

Words and Music by Jim Croce

Additional Lyrics

2. And we've been hidin' from somethin' that should have never gone this far.
   But after all, it's what we've done that makes us what we are.

Chorus: And you've been talkin' in silence. Well, if it's silence you adore,
   Oh, there'll be one less set of footsteps on your floor in the mornin'.

3. But tomorrow's a dream away; today has turned to dust.
   Your silver tongue has turned to clay and your golden rule to rust.

Chorus: If that's the way that you want it, well, that's the way I want it more.
   'Cause there'll be one less set of footsteps on your floor in the mornin'.

Operator
(That's Not the Way It Feels)

Words and Music by Jim Croce

knew well and some-times hat - ed.
I thought _ would save me. _____
dime.

Chorus

Is - n't that the way ____ they _ say it goes? ____ But let's for -

get all that, ___ and give me the num - ber, if you can find ___ it, so

I can ___ call just to tell them I'm fine and to show _____

I've o - ver - come the blow. I've learned to take it well. ___ I on - ly wish my words _

____ could just con - vince my - self that it just was - n't real, _

Play 3 times

_____ but that's not the way it feels.

Photographs and Memories

Words and Music by Jim Croce

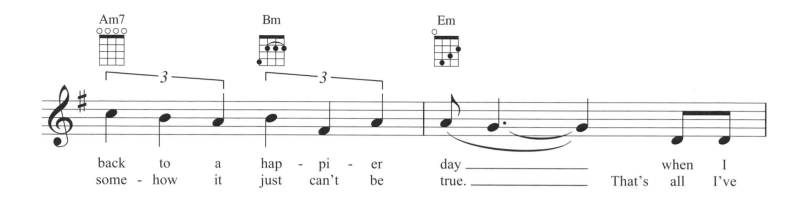

back to a hap - pi - er day _____ when I
some - how it just can't be true. _____ That's all I've

Chorus

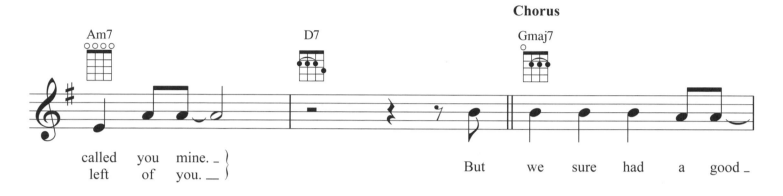

called you mine. _
left of you. _   But we sure had a good _

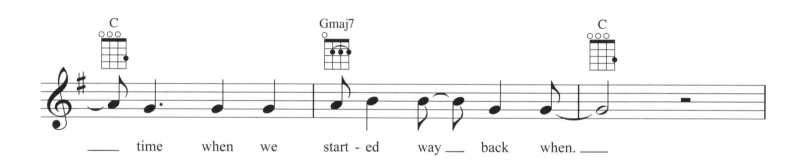

_____ time when we start - ed way _ back when. _____

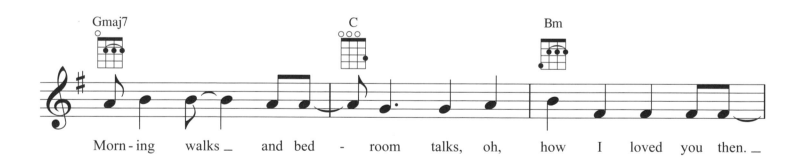

Morn - ing walks _ and bed - room talks, oh, how I loved you then. _

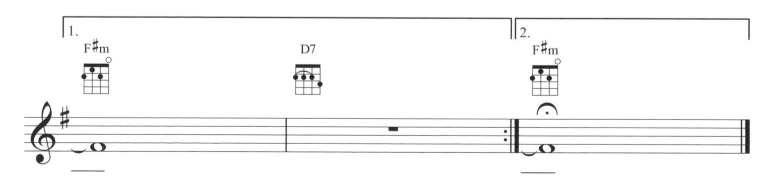

31

Rapid Roy
(The Stock Car Boy)

Words and Music by Jim Croce

First note

Chorus
With a driving beat

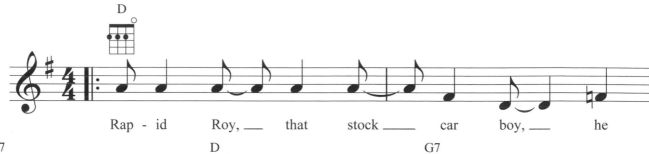

Rap - id   Roy, ___   that   stock ___   car   boy, ___   he

too much   to ___   be - lieve. ___   You know, he   al - ways got   an   ex - tra pack of

cig - a - rettes   rolled up ___   in his   T - shirt   sleeve. ___   He got a

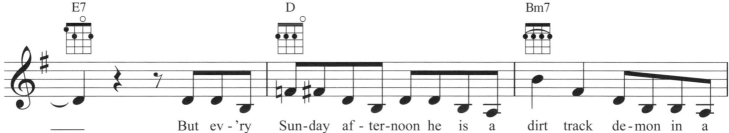

tat - too   on his   arm that say "Ba -   by,"   he got an - oth - er   one that just say   "Hey." ___

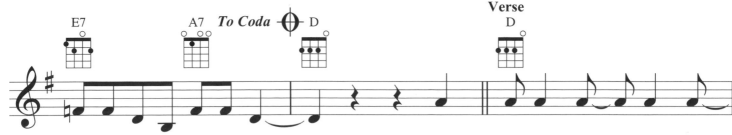

___   But ev - 'ry   Sun - day af - ter - noon he   is a   dirt track   de - mon in a

Fif - ty - sev - en   Chev - ro - let. ___   1. Oh,   Rap - id   Roy, ___   that   stock ___
2. Oh,   Roy so   cool, ___   that   rac -

Roller Derby Queen

Words and Music by Jim Croce

D.S. al Coda

Round 'n' round.   3. Well, I

Outro

Coda

down in the a - re - na. _____   Round 'n' round,   go __

_____ round 'n' round.   Round 'n' round,   go _____ round 'n' round.

Round 'n' round.

Additional Lyrics

2. She's-a five foot six and two fifteen,
   A bleached blonde mama with a streak of mean.
   She knew how to knuckle
   And she knew how to scuffle and fight.
   And the roller derby program said
   That she were built like a 'frigerator with a head.
   The fans called her "Tuffy,"
   But all her buddies called her "Spike."

3. Well, I could not help it but to fall in love
   With this heavy-duty woman I been speakin' of.
   Things looked kind of bad
   Until the day she skated into my life.
   Well, she might be nasty, she might be fat,
   But I never met a person who would tell her that.
   She's my big, blonde bomber,
   My heavy-handed Hackensack Mama.

Workin' at the Car Wash Blues

Words and Music by Jim Croce

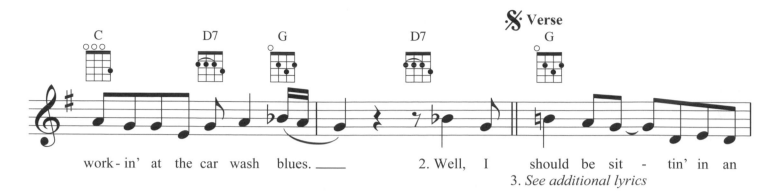

work-in' at the car wash blues. ____ 2. Well, I should be sit - tin' in an
3. *See additional lyrics*

air con - di - tioned of - fice in a swiv - el chair, ____

talk - in' some trash to the sec - re - tar - ies, say- in', "Here, now, ma - ma, come on o - ver

here." In - stead, I'm stuck here rub - bin' these fen - ders with a rag ____ and

walk - in' home in sog - gy old shoes ____ with them stead - i - ly de - press - in', low -

- down, _ mind - mess - in' work- in' at the car wash blues. ____ You know, a

Additional Lyrics

3. Well, all I can do is-a shake my head; you might not believe that it's true.
For workin' at this end of Niagara Falls is an undiscovered Howard Hughes.
So, baby, don't expect to see me with no double martini in any high-brow society news,
'Cause I got them steadily depressin', low-down, mind-messin' workin' at the car wash blues.

These Dreams

Words and Music by Jim Croce

Chorus

What came be - tween us? May - be we were just too young to know, but now and then I feel ___ the same. ___

(Instrumental) And some - times at night I think I hear you call - ing my name. ___ Mm, mm, mm, ___ these dreams, they keep me go - in' these days. ___

Time in a Bottle

Words and Music by Jim Croce

be e-nough time ___ to do the things you want to do once you

find them. I've

looked a-round e-nough ___ to know ___ that you're the one I

want to go through time with.

To Coda

D.S. al Coda
(take 2nd ending)

3. If

Coda

Additional Lyrics

2. If I could make days last forever,
   If words could make wishes come true,
   I'd save ev'ry day like a treasure
   And then again I would spend them with you.

3. If I had a box just for wishes
   And dreams that had never come true,
   The box would be empty except for the mem'ry
   Of how they were answered by you.

Walkin' Back to Georgia

Words and Music by Jim Croce

still a - round, __ I'm gon - na set - tle down __ with that a
still a - round, __ I'm gon - na set - tle down __ with that a
still a - round, __ I'm gon - na set - tle down __ with you, my

hard - lov - in' Geor - gia girl.
hard - lov - in' Geor - gia girl.
hard - lov - in' Geor - gia girl.

Hm, _____ hm, _____

To Coda

hm. _____

Bridge

Geor - gia, can't you hear me call - in'? _____ I'll be home in __ just a while. __

__ And if I had to, I'd __ be crawl - in' just to

D.S. al Coda

Coda

share an - oth - er morn - in' __ smile. __ But you're the

You Don't Mess Around with Jim

Words and Music by Jim Croce

First note

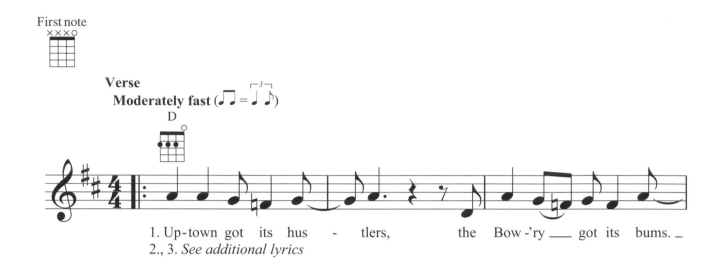

1. Up-town got its hus - tlers, the Bow-'ry ___ got its bums. ___
2., 3. *See additional lyrics*

For - ty - sec - ond Street got big ___ Jim ___ Walk- er. He a

pool - shoot - in' son of a gun. Yeah, he big ___ and ___ dumb ___ as a man ___

___ can come, ___ but he's strong - er than a coun - try horse. ___ And when the

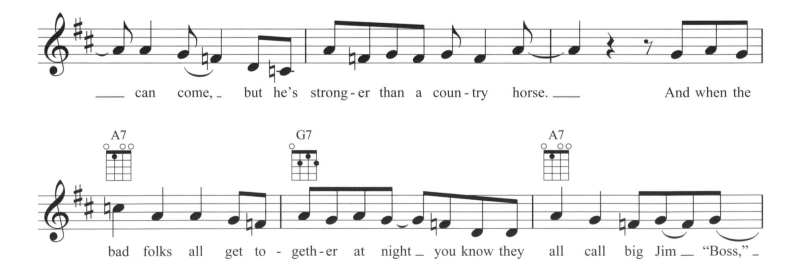

bad folks all get to - geth - er at night ___ you know they all call big Jim ___ "Boss," ___

just ___ be - cause. ___ And they say, ___ "You don't

%. Chorus

tug on Su - per - man's cape, you don't spit in - to the wind, ___

___ you don't pull the mask off that old Lone Ran - ger, and you

don't mess a - round with ___ {1., 2. Jim." _____ 3., 4. Slim." _____} A doo 'n' doo da da Hm. _____

1., 2.

To Coda ⊕

dee dee 'n' dee dee dee. 2. Well, out of 3. Well, a hush___

3. Interlude

Spoken: Yeah, Big Jim got his hat. Find out where it's at. It's not hustlin'

people strange   to you.   Even if you do   got a two -

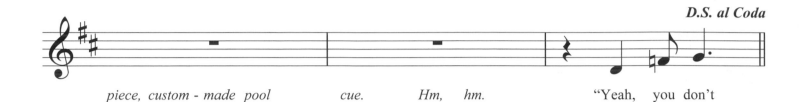

D.S. al Coda

piece, custom - made pool   cue.   Hm, hm.   "Yeah, you don't

Outro

Coda   D

Hm. _____

Repeat and fade

Hm. _____

Additional Lyrics

2. Well, out of south Alabama come a country boy. He said, "I'm lookin' for a man named Jim.
   I am a pool-shootin' boy. My name is Willie McCoy, but down home they call me Slim.
   Yeah, I'm lookin' for the king of Forty-second Street. He drivin' a drop-top Cadillac.
   Last week he took all my money and it may sound funny, but I come to get my money back."
   And everybody say, "Jack, woo, don't you know that you don't…

3. Well, a hush fell over the pool room till Jim, he come boppin' in off the street.
   And when the cuttin' was done, the only part that wasn't bloody was the soles of the big man's feet.
   Yeah, he was cut in about a hundred places and he was shot in a couple more.
   And you better believe I sung a different kind of story when big Jim hit the floor.
   Oh, yeah, they sing, "You don't…